# The Red Squirrel

## Andrew Tittensor

**BLANDFORD PRESS**
Poole          Dorset

# Contents

| | | | |
|---|---|---|---|
| Introduction | 1 | Food and Feeding | 36 |
| Recognition | 4 | Breeding | 37 |
| Description | 5 | Population | 38 |
| Field Signs | 13 | Predators, Parasites | |
| Distribution | 16 | and Disease | 39 |
| Habitat | 21 | Relations with Man | 39 |
| Behaviour | 32 | Further Study | 42 |

## Illustration Credits

*Cover* Geoffrey Kinns; S. Bisserôt page 3; M. Clark 2, 22, 23; D. Corke 11; S. Dalton/NHPA 2; G. Kinns frontispiece, 6, 7, 43; P. Livesley 14; D. MacCaskill 19, 27, 43; D. Smith/Aquilla 34; A. F. Taylor/Aquilla 19; A. Tittensor 10, 11, 22; P. Wayre/NHPA 6; P. D. Wearing/Aquilla 31.

## Picture Editors Michael Clark   David Corke

## Art Work Michael Clark

First published in Great Britain in 1980 by Blandford Press in association with The Mammal Society.

Copyright © 1980 Blandford Press Ltd
Link House, West Street
Poole, Dorset BH15 1LL

ISBN 0 7137 0902 2

**British Library Cataloguing in Publication Data**

Tittensor, Andrew
  The red squirrel.
  1. Eurasian red squirrel – Juvenile Literature
  I. Title    II. Mammal Society
  599'.3232          QL737.R68

*All rights reserved. No part of this book may be reproduced or transmitted in any form or by any means, electronic or mechanical, including photocopying, recording or any information storage and retrieval system, without permission in writing from the Publisher.*

*Printed in Great Britain by Purnell & Sons Ltd., Paulton (Bristol) and London.*

## Introduction

The red squirrel is one of our most attractive and best loved small mammals, yet the closely related grey squirrel is often regarded as an ugly 'tree rat' and an object of hatred. Both are tree-living squirrels, included in the group of mammals known as rodents. There are also many sorts of ground-living and flying squirrels in other parts of the world. This book sets out to describe the red squirrel, its habits and habitat, and to discuss the interaction between red and grey squirrels. It suggests ways of finding and studying red squirrels, and provides some information on their conservation and control.

'Red squirrel' is the usual name for our native squirrel, but alternative names include 'common squirrel', 'brown squirrel', 'light-tailed squirrel', or even 'con', a Scots and northern English word of unknown origin. There are numerous dialect variations of 'squirrel', such as 'skug' and 'skurel'. The name 'squirrel' is derived from an ancient Greek word meaning 'shade tail'. The scientific (Latin) name *Sciurus vulgaris* was given by the famous biologist Linnaeus in 1758 from a specimen at Uppsala in Sweden. The unique British race of the red squirrel was first described by Kerr in 1792, and named *Sciurus vulgaris leucourus.* The 'grey squirrel' or 'eastern gray squirrel', *Sciurus carolinensis,* has been introduced from North America to our islands, but does not occur elsewhere in Europe.

There is popular belief that the red squirrel is virtually extinct in Britain. This is not so, but its most recent decline has been mainly in central and southern England. Elsewhere, especially in large coniferous plantations, it has maintained itself or even increased its range. The possible role of the grey squirrel in this decline is a matter of considerable controversy. After the last Ice Age, when Scots pine forests covered most

**Frontispiece**
*The native red squirrel* (Sciurus vulgaris)—*its sleek appearance, bushy tail and prominent ear tufts are characteristic, but the coat colour varies with the season.*

*The introduced grey squirrel (Sciurus carolinensis)—its heavier build, bushy tail and lack of ear tufts are characteristic, but the coat colour varies with season.*

*These museum skins show the coat colour variation in British red squirrels. Apart from the normal season differences, a dark type with continental influences and an aberrant albino type are included.*

*This red squirrel shows the bleached tail and ear tufts which are typical of the British race (S. vulgaris leucourus) in summer coat, hence the name 'light-tailed squirrel'.*

of Britain and Ireland, red squirrels would have been extremely common. When the British Isles were separated from continental Europe, and the climate became warmer and wetter, mixed deciduous woodlands dominated by oak and lime replaced the pines everywhere except in the Highlands of Scotland. The red squirrel adapted to this new but less suitable type of woodland and survived through from prehistoric times to the present day, though with considerable ups and downs in between.

Another popular belief which has no truth in it whatsoever is that the red squirrel hibernates in winter. It does not hibernate anywhere in its range, not even in the extreme cold of the northern forests of Scandinavia or Russia. It spends longer periods in its nest or drey in winter but will starve if it does not come out to feed. In fact none of the tree-living squirrels hibernate in the way that hedgehogs, bats or dormice do. Hibernating animals become motionless and lower their body temperature, depending entirely upon their internal fat reserves to survive the winter.

**Recognition**

If you live in North Wales, northern Britain or Ireland it will be possible to find red squirrels; otherwise you will probably have to travel. Squirrels are diurnal, which means they sleep at night and are active in daylight. It is best to search for them during the summer months, soon after dawn on a fine day, looking *down* for their feeding signs and *up* for their dreys or the animals themselves. If you are quiet and still during intervals of walking you will hear squirrels 'chucking', moving and feeding in the branches, or perhaps see one leaping between trees or rapidly climbing a trunk.

The red squirrel can be recognised by the following

features: it lives in trees and is about the size of a rat, with a very bushy tail; typically it has a chestnut red coat above, sharply separated from the white fur below, though the coat is greyer in winter and individuals can vary from almost black to pale ashy brown. Close examination shows it has long ear tufts for most of the year, an obvious difference from the grey squirrel where they are more or less absent. When feeding it often squats on its haunches, holding food in its front paws, while its tail is arched over its back; when moving, its tail is stretched out behind as it leaps between branches.

In the British Isles there are few other mammals with which a red squirrel could be confused. The smaller size, colour differences and long ear tufts usually separate it with ease from the grey squirrel, which does show some chestnut red in the summer coat but only quite exceptionally does it have a uniform chestnut coat like the red squirrel (in such a case the extra size and lack of ear tufts distinguishes the grey). The smaller edible dormouse (*Glis glis*) also climbs trees, but has only been introduced to the Chilterns area of England, and is greyish-brown and comes out at night. The brown coloured pine marten (*Martes martes*), once common throughout the British Isles, now occurs only in the northern and western coniferous forests of Britain and in Ireland. It is an agile tree climber too but very much larger than the red squirrel and has prominent ears, a very long bushy tail and a yellowish throat patch. The stoat (*Mustela erminea*) occasionally climbs trees but its tail is not bushy and has an obvious black tip.

**Description**
The appearance of the British red squirrel varies

*Red squirrel on Scots pine.*

*Red squirrel without ear tufts—these are gradually lost through spring and summer as individual hairs are shed.*

**Fig. 1** *Body dimensions of the red squirrel.*

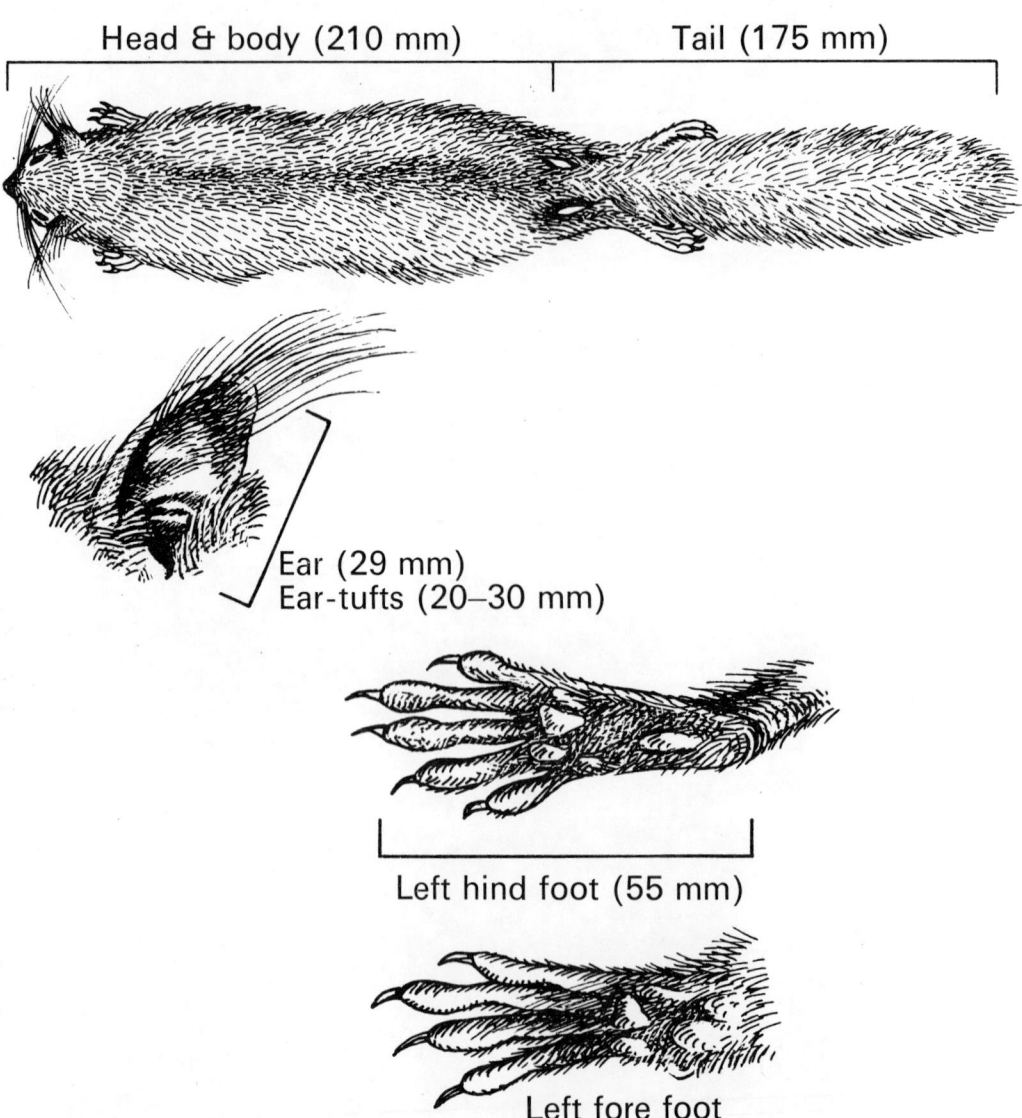

during the year. The *summer coat* is chestnut red above and white below; the ear tufts are sparse and pale or absent and the tail thin, coloured creamy white, buff or reddish-brown. The *winter coat* is red-brown tinged with grey above and white below; the ear tufts are thick, long and brown and the tail dense, dark brown or black. The full-grown *male and female coats* are alike at both seasons, while the *young coat* is redder than the adult's but otherwise similar; it moults to the appropriate seasonal coat after weaning.

The whole winter coat becomes progressively paler as it gradually bleaches, so that the blackish-brown appearance of late autumn turns through red-brown to greyish-brown by the following spring. Most of the fur now moults into the much redder summer coat, but not the ear tufts or the tail hairs which continue to bleach until they become off-white in colour by June or July. They also become much sparser as individual hairs drop out. The whole coat is changed, however, at the autumn moult to complete the cycle. Because of considerable differences in the rate of spread of the bleaching and in the timing of the two moults, there is enormous variation between individual red squirrels in any particular place. Very occasionally all or partially white (albino) varieties are met with in Britain, while all-black (melanistic) and all-red (erythristic) individuals— *including* the normally white underside—are extremely rare; these unusual coat colours are produced when the normal coat colouring process goes wrong.

However, there is another cause of coat colour variation in localised parts of Britain, owing to the added complication of introduced continental races of red squirrel. Our island race is characterised by the bleaching of its ear tufts and tail, and its particular adaptation to Scots pine. At least two continental races have been introduced here by man from Scandinavia

*Typical red squirrel habitat in Sweden—naturally regenerated mixed woodland containing spruce at Öster-Malma in Södermanland.*

*Habitat catastrophe—windblow of Scots pine at Edensmuir Forest in Fife made this woodland unsuitable for red squirrels overnight. Man does the same when he clear-fells a large woodland.*

*Typical red squirrel habitat in Britain—planted coniferous woodland containing pine at Thetford Chase in East Anglia.*

and Western Europe. Unlike our squirrels, their coat does not bleach and they quite normally have two different colour forms: the familiar chestnut red form and a dark brown or black form, each adapted to different types of habitat. These introduced races account for most of the reports of dark-coloured individuals in parts of the British Isles. Note that these dark squirrels still have white undersides, unlike the melanistic varieties mentioned above.

An individual squirrel is heaviest in late summer and autumn, lightest in late winter and spring, but exceptionally well fed or emaciated individuals will be outside the normal weight limits given below:

| | |
|---|---|
| Young appear from drey | 80 to 90 g |
| Young independent | 100 to 150 g |
| Adult females typically | 220 to 355 g |
| Adult males typically | 230 to 435 g |

The grey squirrel is only one-third longer but twice the weight of the red squirrel. The red squirrel's front teeth (incisors) are constantly worn away at their tip as the squirrel gnaws its food, but are continuously replaced from the base. There are no canines—the large teeth for tearing meat that you see in a dog—only a gap. The cheek teeth (premolars and molars) are very important for chewing the food; the lower ones have large hollows on the surface, the upper ones have prominent points and ridges. A new-born squirrel has no teeth, of course, while it suckles the mother. When three weeks old the first teeth appear, but there is no milk set as such, because only some of the cheek teeth are replaced. The older the squirrel is, the more worn are its cheek teeth, and this can be used as a guide to its age.

Squirrels show a number of adaptations to their life in the trees. The hind limbs are extra long and heavy to produce a powerful leap, while the rest of the skeleton is light. The whole of the foot is placed on the surface when moving, and the toes are all long (except the front two thumbs which are tiny), each with a long curved claw to help the squirrel grip or hang on to a branch or trunk. The tail, quite obviously, is large and helps with balance. The tail hairs can be fluffed out by special muscles, and this along with the spreadeagled legs and loose skin on the squirrel's side means it can maintain height during a leap.

**Field Signs**
It is often difficult to see red squirrels themselves, even when conditions appear suitable. However, a good detective can spot their presence from certain signs. Up above the most obvious signs are the spherical leaf nests or dreys (about 30 cm in diameter) made of twigs, leaves and moss, without a special entrance hole, and most often built against the main trunk of a conifer tree at least 3 m above the ground. Down below, the best signs to look for are the throwaways from the squirrels' meals. Red squirrels' main foods are conifer seeds, hidden underneath the scales of pine, spruce and other cones. A squirrel has to remove these scales to get at the tiny seeds. Each seed has a transparent wing which is discarded along with the clean-cut scales and the remaining central cone core. All these remnants can be found scattered over a woodland floor where squirrels have been feeding up in the trees, or in small piles where squirrels have been feeding on the ground. Cone cores left by squirrels show clean-cut scale bases, unlike birds which split or splay the scales but leave them attached to the central core.

Red squirrels eat other foods too, so look for the split shells or husks of mast (the fruits of oak, beech and

*Red squirrel in characteristic squatting pose, exhibiting the white fur below.*

other deciduous trees). Toadstools eaten by squirrels show distinct toothmarks; slugs, in contrast, leave irregular holes with slime trails, birds leave obvious peck marks, and mice and voles leave much smaller toothmarks. In spring it is quite common to find short conifer shoots bitten through, shoots with the top eaten off, discarded bud scales, and chewed male pollen cones. Also in spring, the trees may be left with bark peeled back in long, coiled strips where the squirrels have sought the sappy tissue underneath.

If you find squirrel prints in mud or snow you will note that the hind footprints show five toes with claws, but the front footprints only four. There are usually no tail scuffs (unlike rat tracks) because the tail is held out and up. The droppings are small, and because they are scattered they are not easy signs to find for identification.

**Distribution**
The red squirrel occurs over much of Europe (from Ireland and Spain to Scandinavia and the Balkans) and Asia (eastern Russia to North China, Korea and northern Japan), in fact wherever there are suitable trees. In the rest of Japan its place is taken by the similar Japanese squirrel (*Sciurus lis*), while it is replaced round the eastern end of the Mediterranean and the Black Sea by the Persian squirrel (*Sciurus anomalus*).

In Britain the red squirrel is widespread in northern England and much of Scotland, except for the Central Lowlands and far north-west where, of course, there is little tree cover. It occurs in large areas of Wales, but is absent from central and southern England except for a few widely-scattered localities. It is also present throughout most of Ireland, despite the fact that this country has the lowest percentage area of tree cover in

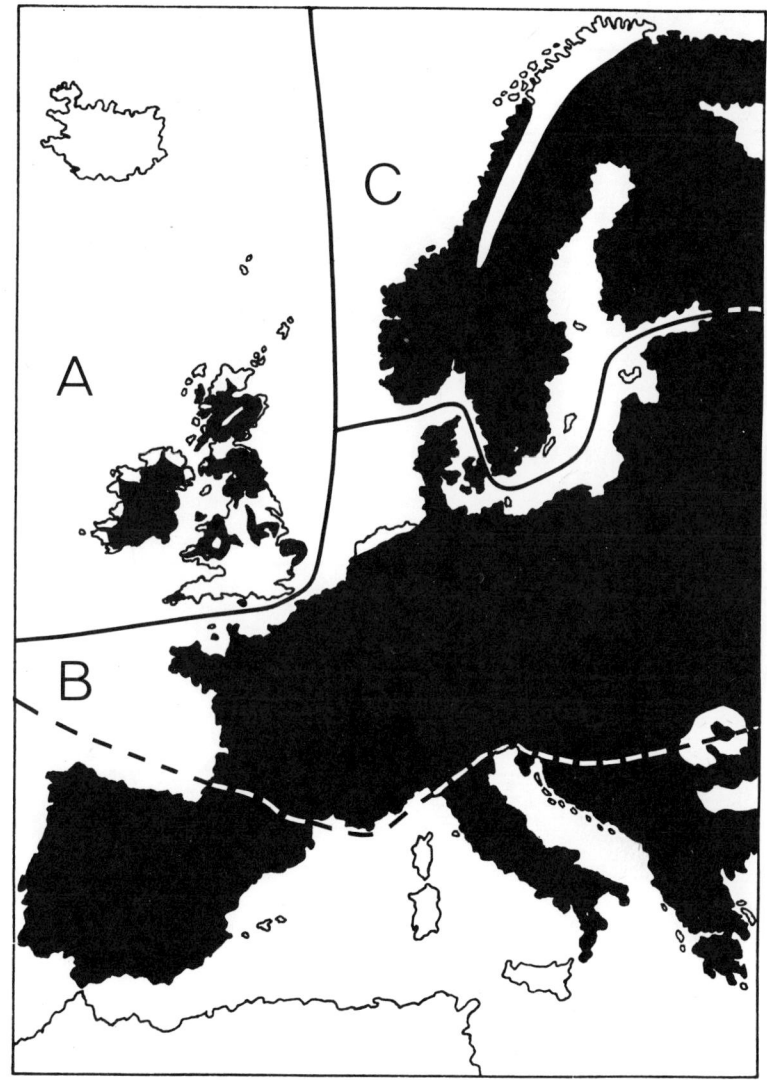

**Fig. 2** *Distribution of red squirrel in Western Europe. The map shows the approximate range of A—the British race, B—the West European race, and C—the Scandinavian race. In addition to our own race, races B & C have been introduced to Britain over the last 200 years, causing greater coat colour variation in certain areas.*

*Red squirrel entering hollow tree for store of acorns.*

*A red squirrel tackling a hazel nut—a hole is nicked in the pointed end before the shell is split in two by the incisor teeth.*

*Cone feeding remains left by a red squirrel on a birch stump at Brecon Forest in Powys. Food is often carried to a raised site before consumption when squirrels are foraging on the ground.*

all Europe except Iceland. The following British offshore islands have red squirrels too: Jersey, Brownsea, Isle of Wight, Anglesey, Arran and Skye.

There have been many changes in the distribution and abundance of the red squirrel in historic times, but there is less information about its very early history. The British squirrel was segregated from its European neighbours about 7000 years ago, and has since developed into a distinct race. It has become particularly adapted to woodlands of Scots pine, which was the only native cone-bearing conifer to reach the British Isles before they were cut-off by the sea. The continental races, however, had several suitable conifers to choose from, including European larch, Norway spruce and silver fir.

Early but sparse evidence from documents, heraldry, carving and place names shows that red squirrels were widespread during historic times in the British Isles, and certainly by the late Medieval period. In Ireland they were extinct by the early eighteenth century and all the present Irish squirrels are descendants of English stock, introduced there between 1815 and 1856. Probably because of extensive destruction of tree cover they were also extinct from southern Scotland by the same period, while in the Scottish Highlands they nearly became extinct in the late eighteenth and early nineteenth centuries, again due to large-scale deforestation. Scotland was repopulated with English squirrels, introduced between 1772 and 1872, though a few also came from continental Europe. In England and Wales the change from natural woodland cover to an open agricultural landscape took place much earlier, between Roman and Medieval times, so it is likely that red squirrels declined then, though no written records survive to confirm this.

Between 1860 and 1900 there was a superabundance

of red squirrels throughout Britain and Ireland, probably a result of the extensive new plantations of foreign conifers which had become fashionable earlier that century. Red squirrels became such serious forestry pests that 'Squirrel Clubs' were formed to attempt control. Soon after 1900 there was a sudden decline, probably due to large-scale felling of the now mature trees (accelerated by First World War timber demands) and accompanied by epidemic disease. Control methods were not responsible: they had been producing little effect for the previous four decades.

Red squirrel numbers started to increase again earlier this century and by the 1930s they were common but not abundant. They were not able to return to all their previous localities which were now occupied by the grey squirrel (introduced from 1876 onwards but not widespread until the 1920s) which could use deciduous woodlands to better advantage. There followed the second decline of the century and over quite large areas of southern Britain the red squirrel has become extinct since the 1940s, leaving behind small isolated populations. Its future, if its past is anything to go by, may not be wholly bleak in England and Wales, especially if the general public's attitude to large coniferous plantations improves! Indeed, the spread of conifer plantations (of both native and introduced species) and their maturation in the mid-twentieth century, has recently allowed the red squirrel to expand into new parts of Scotland.

**Habitat**
Red squirrels are most abundant in large and continuous areas of mature coniferous forest, whether these originate by planting or from natural regeneration. This is because the species is particularly adapted to such woodland, using conifers as its main food source,

*A red squirrel collecting a larch cone from slender branches before carrying it back to a more secure feeding spot towards the centre of the tree.*

*Red squirrel feeding signs on Scots pine cones—stripped green cone cores. They start on the new green cone crop in late June or July, and continue feeding on them as they turn brown through to seedfall next spring—a period of nine to eleven months.*

*Red squirrel drey built high up against the trunk of a pine tree. It is made of a framework of interwoven twigs, lined with grass, moss, and other soft material.*

as cover for its nest sites, and as shelter (from animals which eat squirrels) in the form of aerial routeways up in the canopy. Red squirrels are also abundant in extensive mixed woodlands containing a large proportion of conifers. Deciduous woods, immature and overmature woods, small copses and sparsely wooded areas of all types are secondary habitats, providing less stable conditions for survival and thus usually supporting fewer squirrels. Such habitats are typically occupied by overflow populations from the favoured areas when times are good, but under adverse conditions the red squirrel retreats to its primary coniferous habitat.

In continental Europe there is a much wider choice of woodland type available to squirrels compared with the British Isles. In addition, it seems that the continental 'dark' form predominates in spruce and fir forests and perhaps also in beechwoods, while the 'red' continental form favours pine forests and possibly certain deciduous trees too. In Britain and Ireland, however, there was a restricted choice of woodland type before the recent introduction of foreign trees by man, so our island race of squirrels became adapted to the species-poor natural forests of the Boreal period at around 6000 BC. These consisted of Scots pine with an understorey of hazel; the presence of hazel may help explain the squirrel's survival in the pure deciduous woodland of southern Britain over the past few thousand years, because the Boreal pine forests survive only as remnants in the Scottish Highlands.

A recent complicating factor has been the introduction of grey squirrels to the British Isles, and habitat seems to hold the key to understanding the relationship between the two species. There is no evidence to support the idea that grey squirrels caused the most recent decline of red squirrels in southern Britain—indeed, what evidence there is suggests that it would have occurred anyway, and it was, after all, merely the latest decline in a series of ups and downs. Past fluctuations in numbers were caused by habitat changes, the declines accompanying loss of suitable woodland habitat. In the latest case, however, the grey squirrel filled the vacuum left by the red, moving into those habitats to which it was best suited—deciduous and mixed woodlands—and thus precluding any future return of the red to its former haunts.

It is instructive at this point to look at the situation of the 'eastern gray' squirrel in its native North America. Here the typical habitat is dense deciduous forest, particularly with oak, hickory and walnut, but it also enters the southern edge of the coniferous belt where deciduous trees are mixed in. In pure conifer forest it is replaced by the small American red squirrel *(Tamiasciurus hudsonicus)* while in the smaller woodlots and scattered trees of hedgerow, park and garden it is replaced by a third species, the larger fox squirrel (*Sciurus niger*). In Britain the grey squirrel is now occupying the same deciduous woodland habitat as in its native country *plus* the small woodland habitat of the fox squirrel. It seems to be at a competitive advantage with our native squirrel in mixed woodland situations where at least 25 per cent of the trees are broadleaved. Thus the red squirrel is becoming restricted to its original primary habitat—large blocks of pure or nearly pure conifer. To form ideal habitat such blocks should contain at least 50 hectares of mature Scots pine (or suitably introduced conifer substitute). Scots pine is sufficiently mature at 25 to 80 years of age, when it gives reliable seed production, drey sites and cover, provided that the trees are close enough to form a continuous canopy.

*Red squirrel eating sapling bark.*

*Red squirrel carrying a larch cone to an elevated feeding site—food items are always carried by mouth, but are held and manipulated by the front feet for eating.*

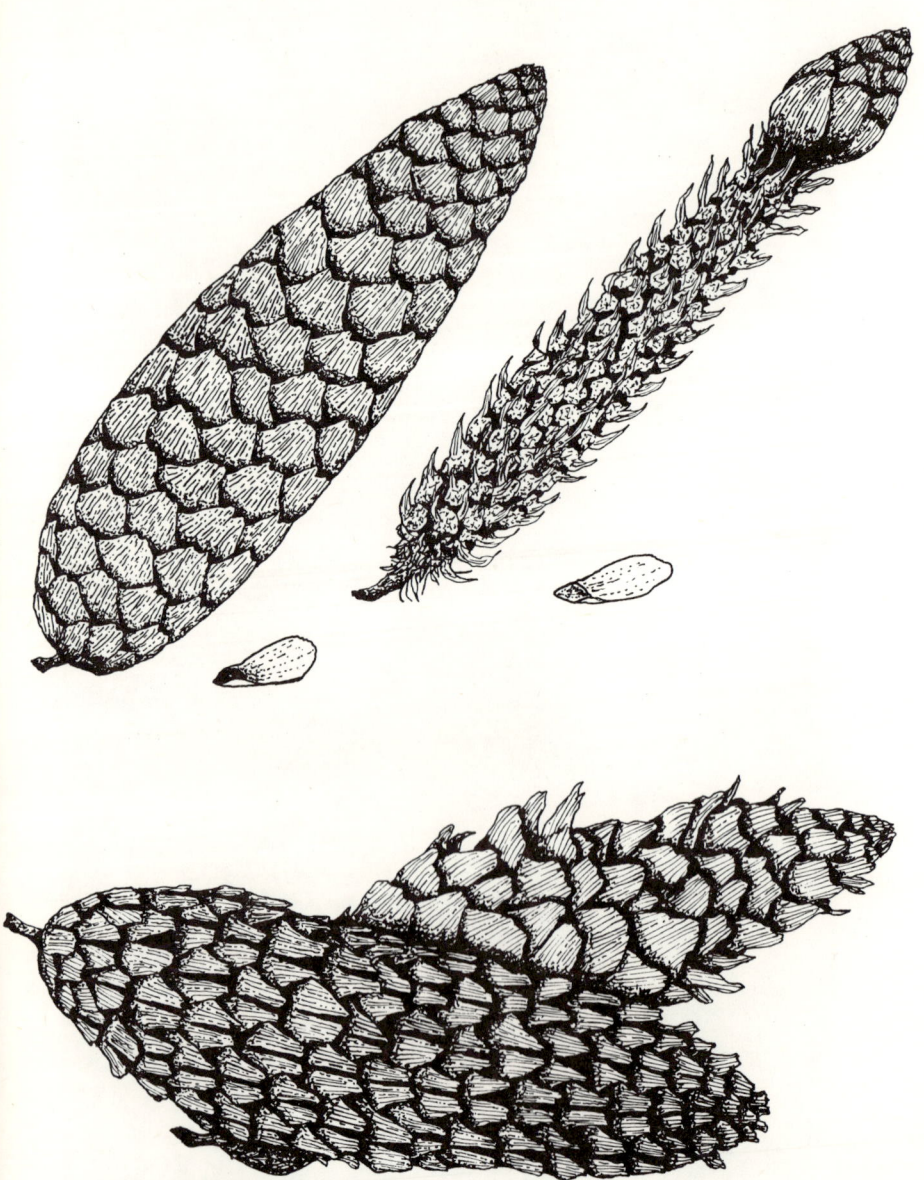

**Fig. 3** *Red squirrel feeding remains of pine (top left) and spruce (top right) cones—note the clean-cut bases of the cone scales left on the central cone core. Even the seed wing is discarded as the tiny seeds are extracted.*
*Bird feeding remains on pine (bottom left) and spruce (bottom right) cones—note the ragged appearance where the cone scales have been split by crossbills (front of pair) or torn by woodpeckers (rear of pair).*

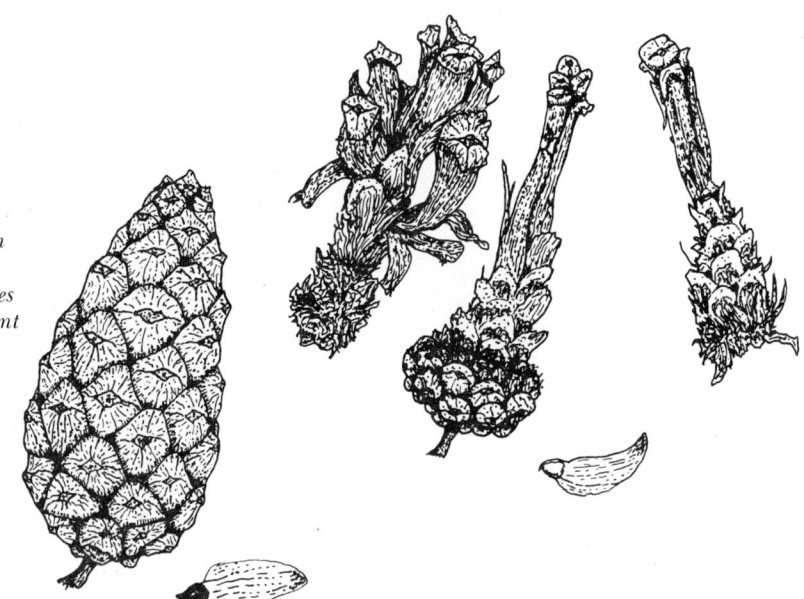
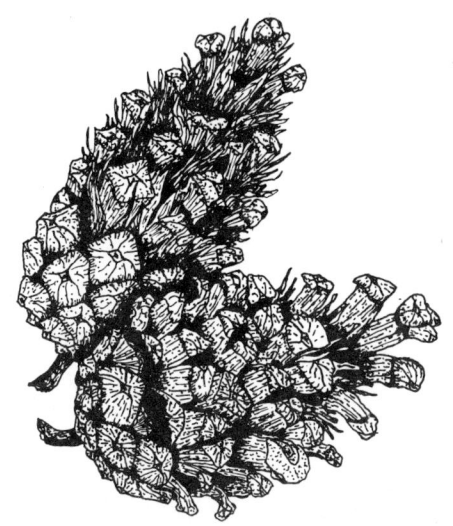

*Red squirrel at ease in ideal habitat.*

*A dark-coated red squirrel in Britain, showing some continental influence, in contrast to the typical British race squirrel shown on page 3.*

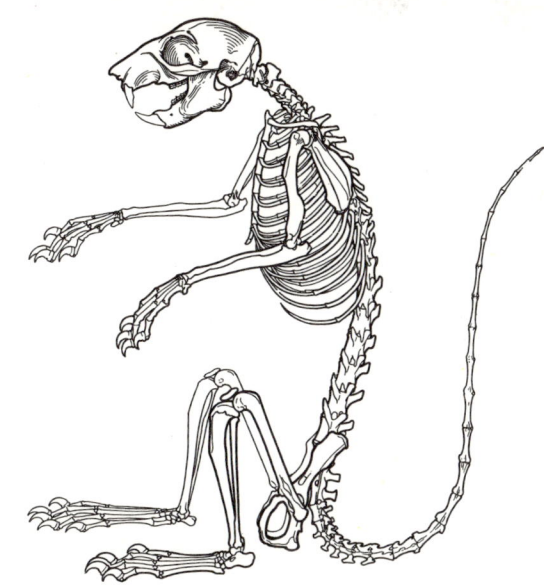

**Fig. 4** *Red squirrel skeleton in erect 'alert' pose—note the light but long limbs, feet and curved claws for climbing and grasping trees. The tail is stretched out behind when leaping and used for balance.*

31

## Behaviour

The red squirrels inhabiting a woodland have a particular pattern of daily activity, with peak periods interspersed with quiet ones. Activity starts half an hour either side of sunrise, and some squirrels can be seen active between then and sunset. In summer there are two peaks of activity, the main one for three to four hours after dawn, and a lesser peak for two to three hours before sunset. As the days shorten towards winter these two peaks gradually merge into one around midday. In between activity bursts the squirrel rests in a drey or on a convenient branch. Away from the drey over half the time is spent searching for and eating food, and the remainder in grooming, escaping from animals which hunt them, or communicating with other squirrels. Strong winds, driving snow, heavy rain and high humidity all reduce activity. If food is scarce then a squirrel has to spend more time searching for it, while foods high in nourishment such as sweet chestnut or pine seeds are needed in smaller quantities than less nourishing green foods.

A squirrel does not roam over the whole of a large woodland, but confines its normal daily activities to a restricted area within the wood, with which it becomes very familiar. We call this area a 'home range', and it overlaps with the ranges of other squirrels, rather than becoming an exclusive and defended territory as is the case with many birds. In a Scottish pine forest the size of a red squirrel's home range was found to average $470 \times 285 \times 15$ m, but this varies in shape and size as food supply or squirrel numbers alter. It must contain all the habitat requirements for the everyday life of a red squirrel: plentiful food, cover from hunting animals and sites for dreys. Dreys may be built anywhere suitable within the home range. Each squirrel usually has several dreys.

The home range is used in a different way through the year. In a Scots pine forest, during autumn and winter the squirrels will be mainly in the tree canopy because the important food—seeds from pine cones—is there. During spring and summer, as the cones open and the seeds drop, more food has to be found on the ground. A deciduous woodland differs because the fallen tree fruits are on the ground in autumn and early winter, whereas in spring and summer much of the available food such as buds or tree pollen is in the branches. Burying tree fruits is a response to food surplus, and they may be hidden in the ground, in tree hollows, or even dreys, usually singly or in small groups. The hidden fruits are found again later by smell and eaten during late winter, when other foods become scarce.

Red squirrels come into contact with each other via their overlapping home ranges and when seeking mates. Throughout the year they can be seen chasing and biting each other, and heard screaming. Squirrels also communicate with each other by body postures, voice and scent. The most characteristic calls are 'chucking' sounds, which may be soft, or harsh and loud accompanied by vigorous tail flicking and foot stamping. Other noises include an explosive 'wrruhh' sound, moans and teeth chattering, while the young have a shrill piping call.

Squirrels have good eyesight with exceptional focussing power and a wide field-of-view to cope with swift movement and jumping; however their colour sense and twilight vision are poor. Their sense of smell is also acute, and is used in finding and choosing food. Touch is enhanced by groups of specially sensitive hairs, which are particularly prominent in young nestlings.

*Two young red squirrels exploring the world outside their breeding drey. Youngsters first begin to emerge at eight or nine weeks old, and have intense red coats.*

## Food and Feeding

Squirrels are herbivores, which means they eat plant material nearly all the time, and the bulk of their diet consists of seeds and fruits making them strictly speaking 'granivores'. They will take a very wide range of foods at different seasons but tree seeds, especially those from Scots pine cones, assorted tree foliage and toadstools make up their staple fare throughout the year in Britain.

It is amazing how adept squirrels are at procuring and extracting seeds from Scots pine cones. A squirrel will select a cone from a pine branch, snip it from its stalk and carry it by mouth to a feeding site near the centre of the tree. Then, either hanging from a branch or squatting on its haunches, the scales are gnawed off in turn starting from the base, as the cone is held by its front feet. Each tiny seed is extracted, its wing removed to blow away, and then eaten. A cone contains about 30 black seeds, tightly placed in pairs beneath the spirally-arranged cone-scales. It may take only two or three minutes for the squirrel to extract and eat all the seed before it discards the cone and searches for another one to repeat the process. By estimating how many cones a red squirrel manages in one day, a simple calculation shows that a typical squirrel gets through 20,000 to 40,000 pine cones in one year. No wonder the throw-away signs give the secretive squirrel away!

Hazel nuts are important food in a deciduous woodland. A skilled adult squirrel holds the blunt end in its front paws and nicks a hole in the pointed end. It then splits the nut in two by inserting its lower front teeth to prise the shell apart so that it can extract and eat the large kernel.

In addition to plants a small amount of animal matter is consumed, including the eggs, young and adults of both insects and birds. The constantly-growing front

**Fig. 5** *Breeding season of the red squirrel in Britain.*

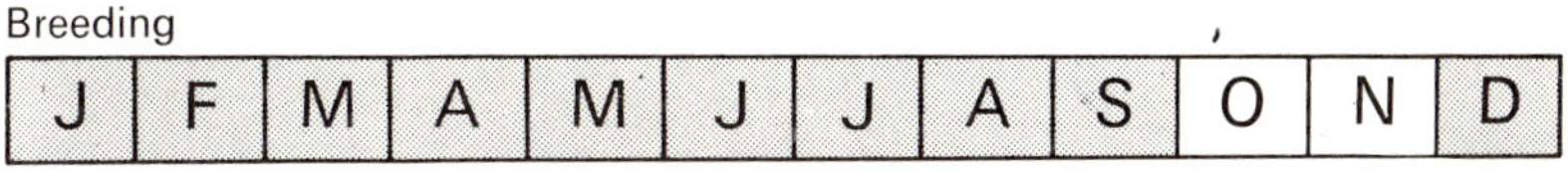

| Breeding | | | | | | | | | | | |
|---|---|---|---|---|---|---|---|---|---|---|---|
| J | F | M | A | M | J | J | A | S | O | N | D |

teeth are trimmed on hard material like bark, stones, bones and antlers but these may also be important sources of minerals. Squirrels do need to drink in exceptionally hot weather, but otherwise they can obtain enough liquid from dew and from their normal foods.

## Breeding

Young squirrels are born between January and September in special thickly-lined dreys. Mature females often produce two litters a year, each of 1 to 6 young, with spring litters concentrated between mid-February and mid-April and summer litters in June and July. However, the breeding season can be delayed by bad weather, and the availability of food during the preceeding winter also influences breeding success. If there was very little food, no young are born that year. If there was only partial failure of the cone crop, the breeding season is reduced to one main litter. This is because the starving females do not put on enough fat to cope with the extra demands of pregnancy and suckling the young. Under normal conditions year old females only produce one litter in their first breeding season.

Squirrels mate after a lengthy courtship which involves 'slow motion' chases and close play—pregnancy lasts about 38 days. The nestlings are born blind, deaf, toothless and naked, and weigh under 15 g. They suckle the mother's milk for 7 weeks before weaning starts. When they are a few days old colouring appears across their back emerging as hair at one week and increasing to a dense coat by 3 weeks. At about this time the lower front teeth come through, though swollen gums can be spotted a week earlier. At 4 weeks their eyes open, followed quickly by their ears and the youngsters now weigh some 50 g. The upper front teeth appear when they are 5 to 6 weeks old, followed by the cheek teeth from 7 weeks onwards as the young begin eating solid food. At 10 weeks all their teeth are through, weaning is over and the youngsters weigh over 100 g. By now the young squirrels are starting to explore the hazardous world outside the drey, but do not become completely independent until they are 4 months old. The breeding season is over by October and the surviving young have started to disperse.

## Population

Red squirrels can reach densities of one adult squirrel for every 1 to 2 hectares of favourable pine habitat, with roughly equal numbers of males and females. Although many young are born each spring and summer, increasing numbers dramatically for a short period, most of them die between birth and the following winter from causes such as starvation, being eaten by predators, disease, accidents and road deaths. With relatively stable squirrel numbers between years, some 20 to 40 per cent of the adult breeding population dies and is replaced by young each year. This rate of replacement of adults by young is well below the normal breeding potential, which even when it is fully achieved means that only 12 to 15 per cent of the year's young survive to join the adult population. Where red squirrels are exploited for food, fur and sport, or controlled as pests, many more young survive to compensate for increased losses of adults. Squirrels surviving to adulthood may live up to 5 or 6 years old, though longer is possible in captivity.

Differences in squirrel numbers between years are influenced in the short-term by food supply, in response to cone crop failure or abundance, but long-term trends reflect the availability of suitable woodland habitat. Man has greatest effect on squirrel numbers by altering or destroying this habitat.

**Predators, Parasites and Disease**
Predators are those animals which eat squirrels as part of their normal food. These include wild cats (*Felis sylvestris*) and pine martens, both of which climb trees, but these are now extinct over much of Britain and so are unimportant predators in these islands. The greatest risk of predation for squirrels today is when they are on the ground, particularly young and inexperienced squirrels who may fall prey to large birds such as the golden eagle (*Aquila chrysaetos*), buzzard (*Buteo buteo*) and goshawk (*Accipiter gentilis*) or mammals like the stoat, fox (*Vulpes vulpes*), domestic cat and dog.

Tiny parasites also eat squirrels, but not usually with such fatal results! These include three species of flea, two sucking lice, and several ticks and mites, which inhabit the squirrel's fur and pierce the skin for blood. There are also numerous internal parasites, including one which causes many squirrels to die from a disease called coccidiosis. Epidemics of mange or scab disease are caused by a virus.

**Relations with Man**
It is because red squirrels are so appealing that a desire

has arisen in Britain to conserve them where they have become rare, and to reintroduce them where they are now extinct. In parts of Europe and Asia they provide food, pelts and hunting sport but in Britain the only commercial use is for their fur which makes good paint brushes for artists and trout flies for fishermen. On the other hand they can become forestry pests, and where serious damage to timber trees occurs it is necessary to control or discourage them. Whatever our attitude towards red squirrels, it becomes necessary to manage their numbers to restore the natural balance when this is upset by man.

Where conservation is our objective, unfortunately there is little that can be done in the short-term. It is only possible to prevent grey squirrels reaching isolated woodlands or islands. However, long-term measures can make the habitat more favourable for red squirrels, and it is best to concentrate such efforts on areas of primary habitat, that is extensive coniferous woodland. The following points should be borne in mind when drawing up a plan for a woodland. It should provide the red squirrel with a large and continuous area of conifer (exceeding 50 hectares and preferably much greater), and this conifer should include a high proportion of Scots pine (or other reliable cone producers). It is best to add in small amounts of other conifer species (in scattered blocks or mixed with the Scots pine) to help reduce the likelihood of complete cone crop failure. At the same time try to keep the deciduous tree content of the wood to a minimum (certainly below 25%, and preferably under 1%) resisting the urge to plant amenity belts at the edges. It is particularly important that most of the trees should be mature (for Scots pine between 25 and 80 years old) to provide reliable cone crops, secure drey sites, limb-free trunks and continuous aerial routeways. By planting young trees at intervals, a continuous supply of mature trees will be provided for the future. These trees should be gradually thinned out to avoid the instability caused by clear-felling all the trees at once.

If you are considering reintroducing red squirrels where they have become extinct, think about the following points before you start. Ensure that they are not likely to cause future problems with tree damage, and consult neighbouring landowners fully. Ensure that the introduced squirrels come from British rather than continental European stock (this is to safeguard the unique nature of our island race). Ensure that taking the squirrels is not going to deplete an area where they are on the decline, and finally ensure the proposed area of reintroduction contains suitable habitat (at least 50 hectares of mature conifer).

Red squirrels damage trees in several ways, but the most serious is their habit of stripping bark from the main trunk to reach the juicy tissue below. As these wounds heal over calluses are formed so that the timber is of poor quality and strength. Sometimes the whole trunk is girdled of bark, causing the tree tip to die back and the top of the tree is liable to blow out in high winds. The main trees attacked include Scots pine, European larch, lodgepole pine and Norway spruce. The worst period of damage is from May to July. Where control measures (shooting, drey poking or cage trapping) are necessary they should be concentrated in the period immediately before and during damage, and confined to areas of 'at-risk' woodland only. This is only a short-term solution, attempting to reduce squirrel numbers temporarily over a limited area, and thereby reducing damage. In the long-term it is possible to plan forestry operations in a commercial woodland to make the habitat less favourable to red squirrels.

**Further Study**
With so few studies of red squirrels, new observations and discoveries can be of great interest. Before embarking on such a study read all the books and leaflets on the subject that you can find through your local library, and obtain the permission and goodwill of the landowner whose woods you wish to visit. Any field study of a wild mammal is exciting and rewarding, provided accurate records are kept in a notebook. There is little equipment needed, though binoculars may help observations, but the ability to get up at dawn is of paramount importance! You can learn a lot from studying signs, so do not be downhearted if you cannot actually see squirrels.

Although it is perfectly legal to keep red squirrels in captivity, before you do so consider carefully whether you could do your studies in another manner, and especially whether you are depleting an already 'at-risk' wild population by taking the squirrels. Remember that they need a very large outdoor cage with raised nest boxes, branches for jumping and a constant supply of cones, nuts, maize or other seeds for food. They are easier to rear if taken when very young, but require constant attention at first.